I0480916

Hippie Trippy Coloring Experience

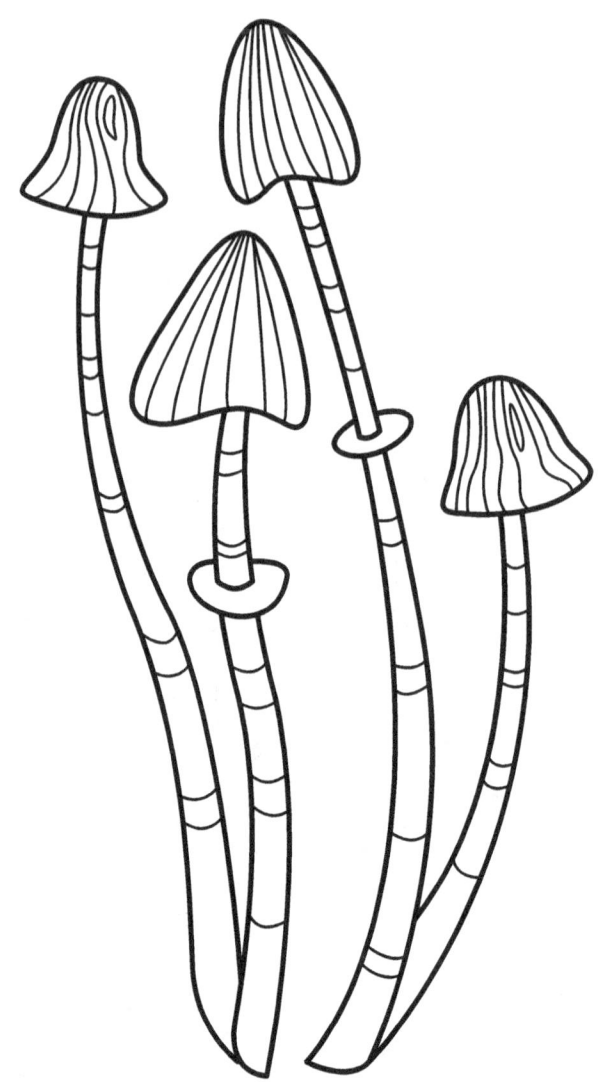

This book belongs to...

....

....

....

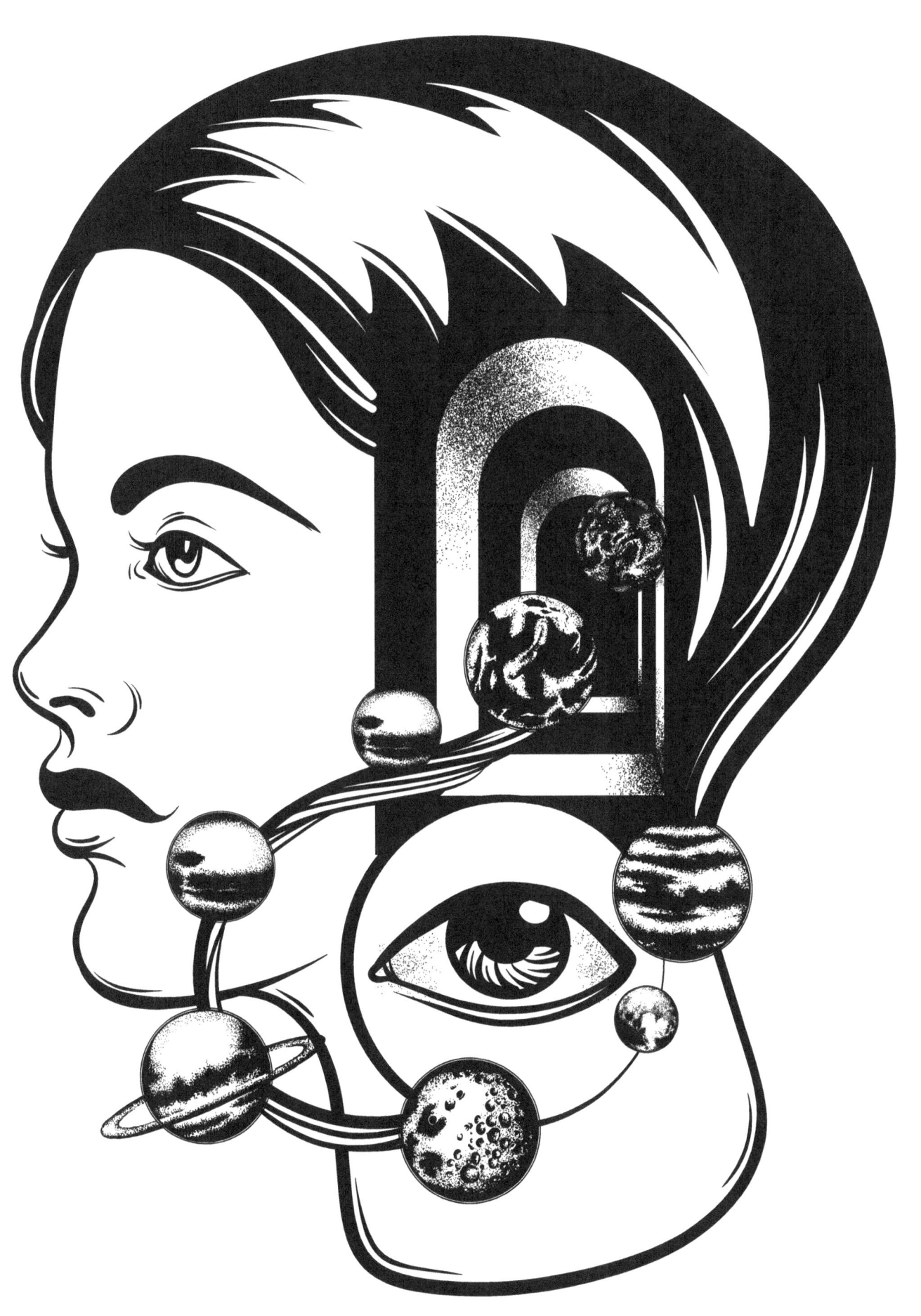

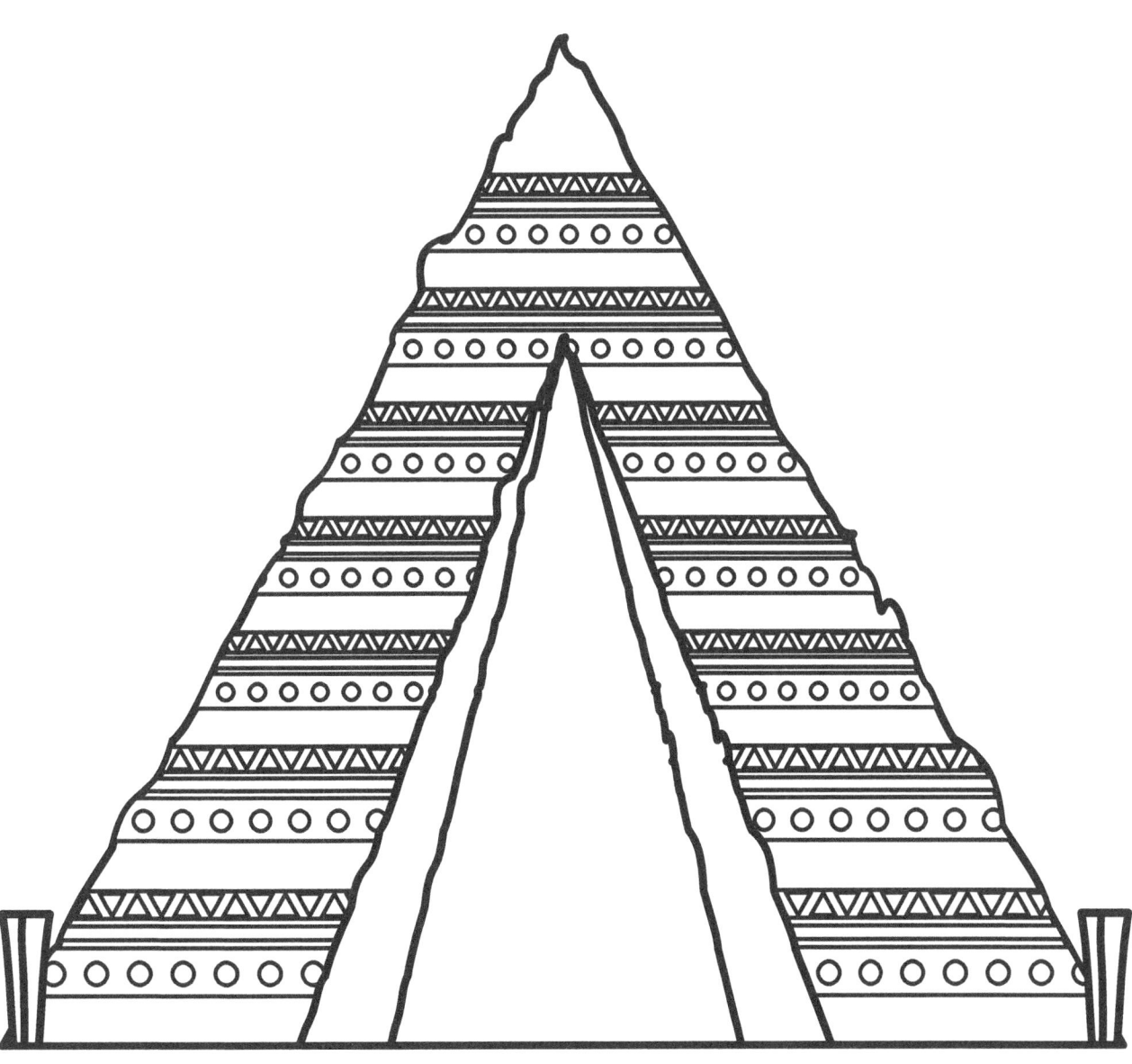

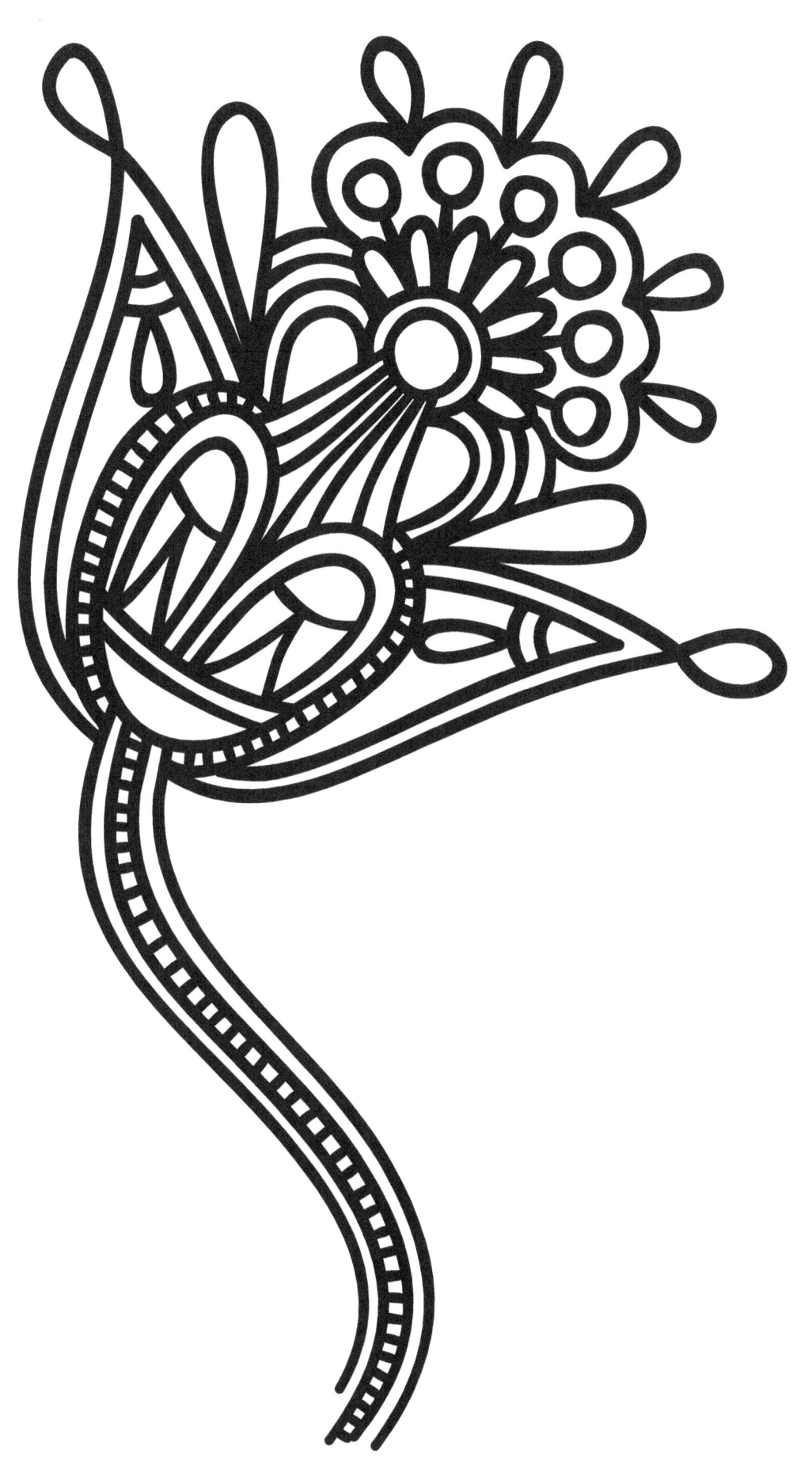

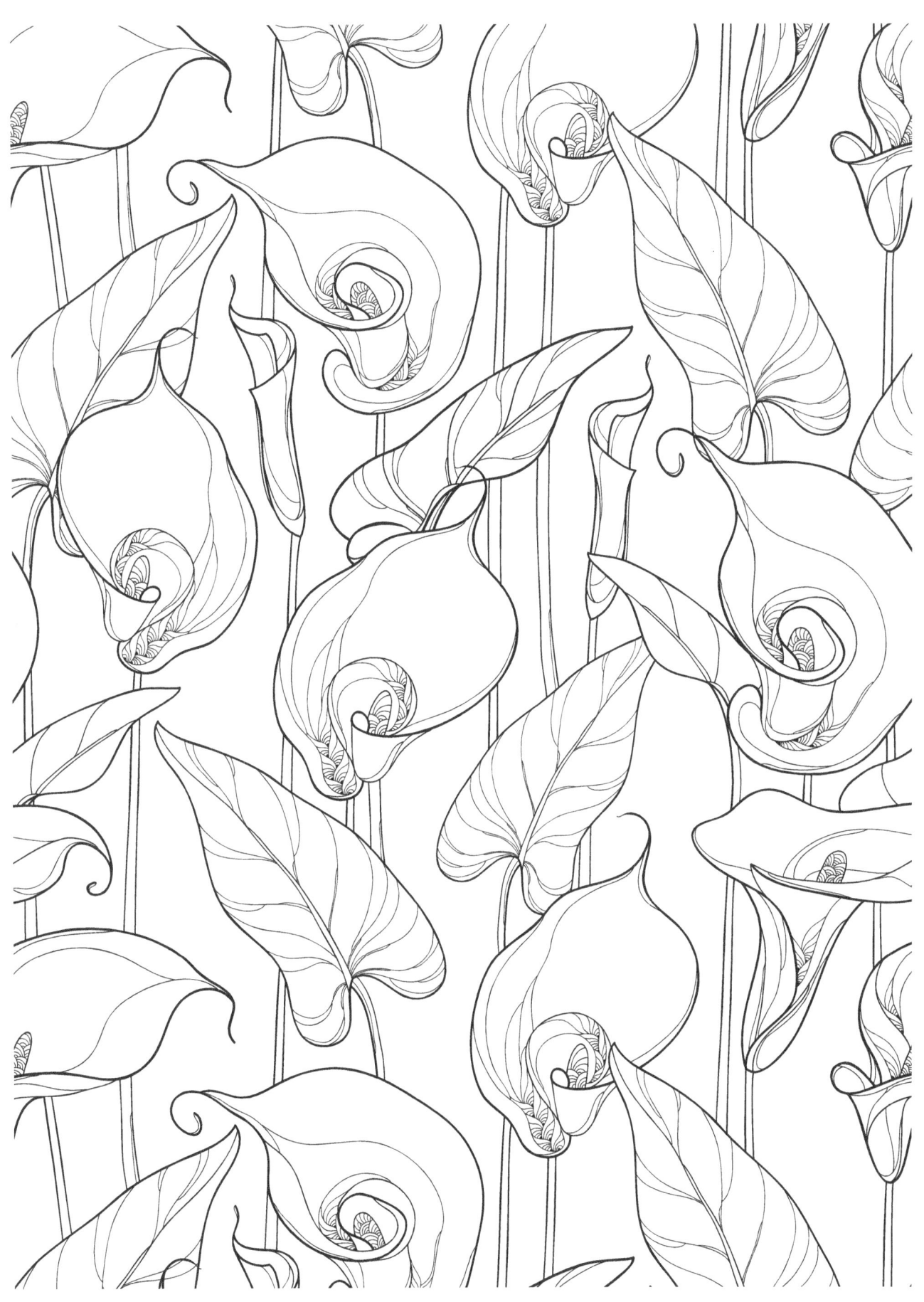

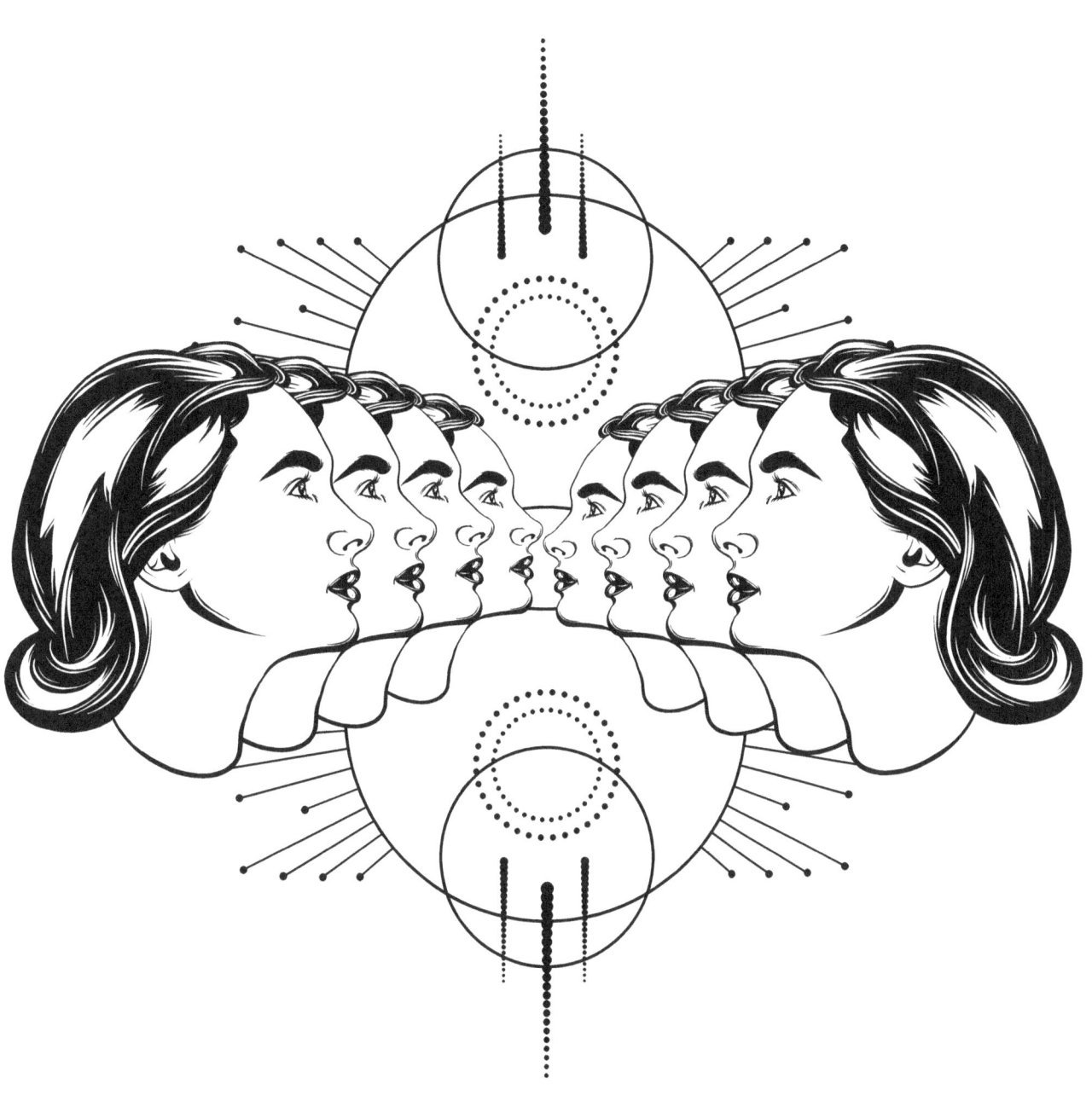

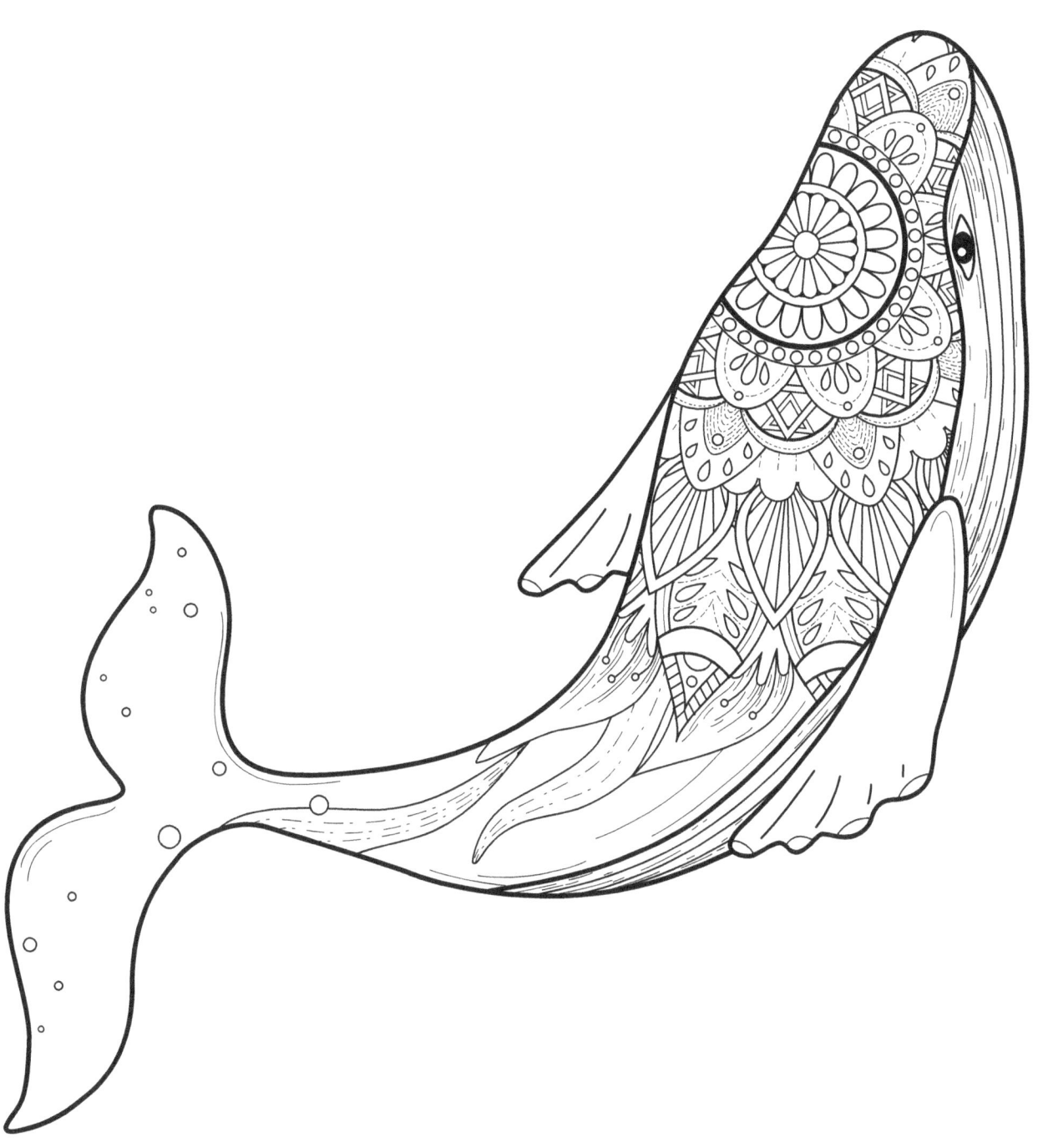

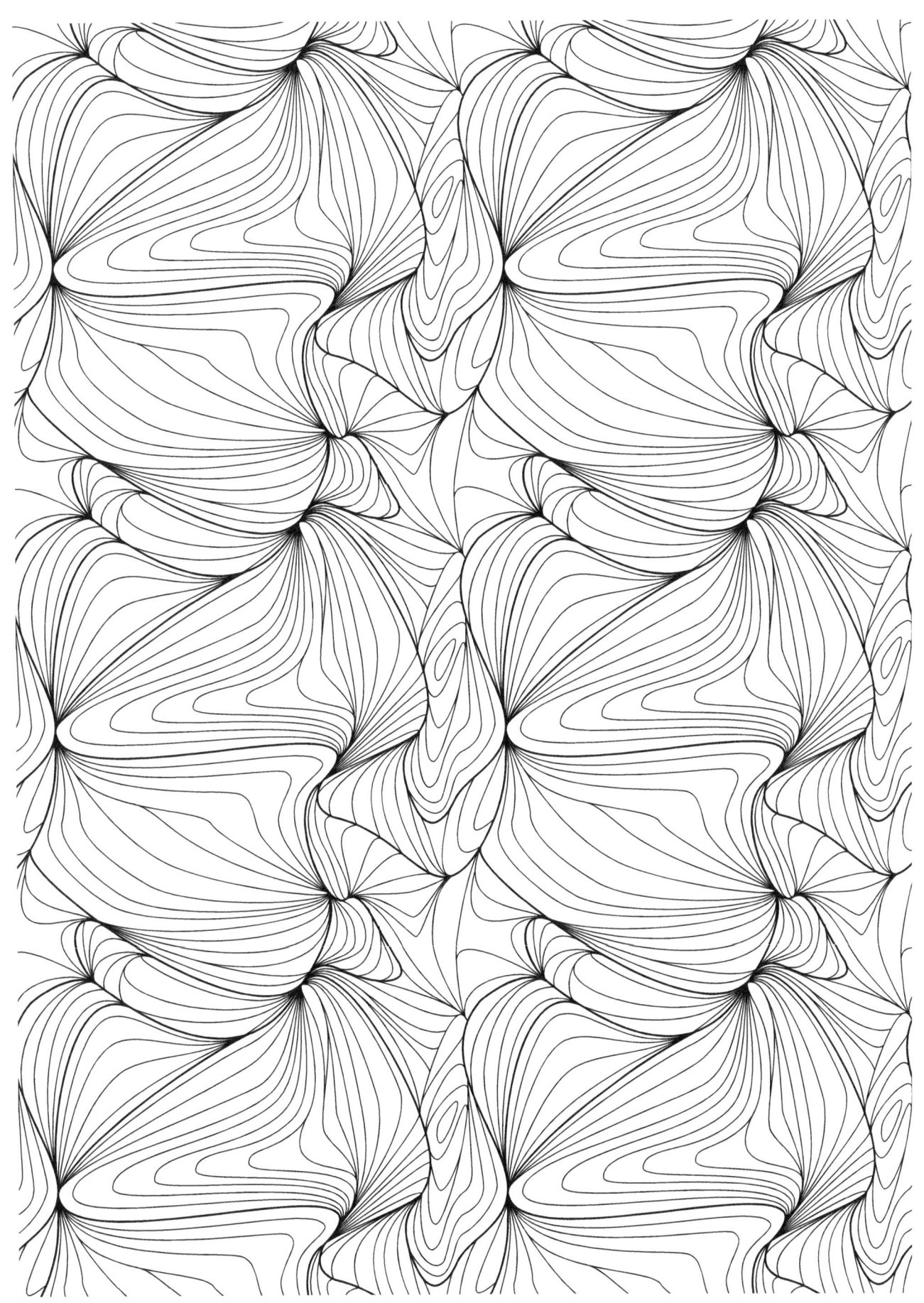

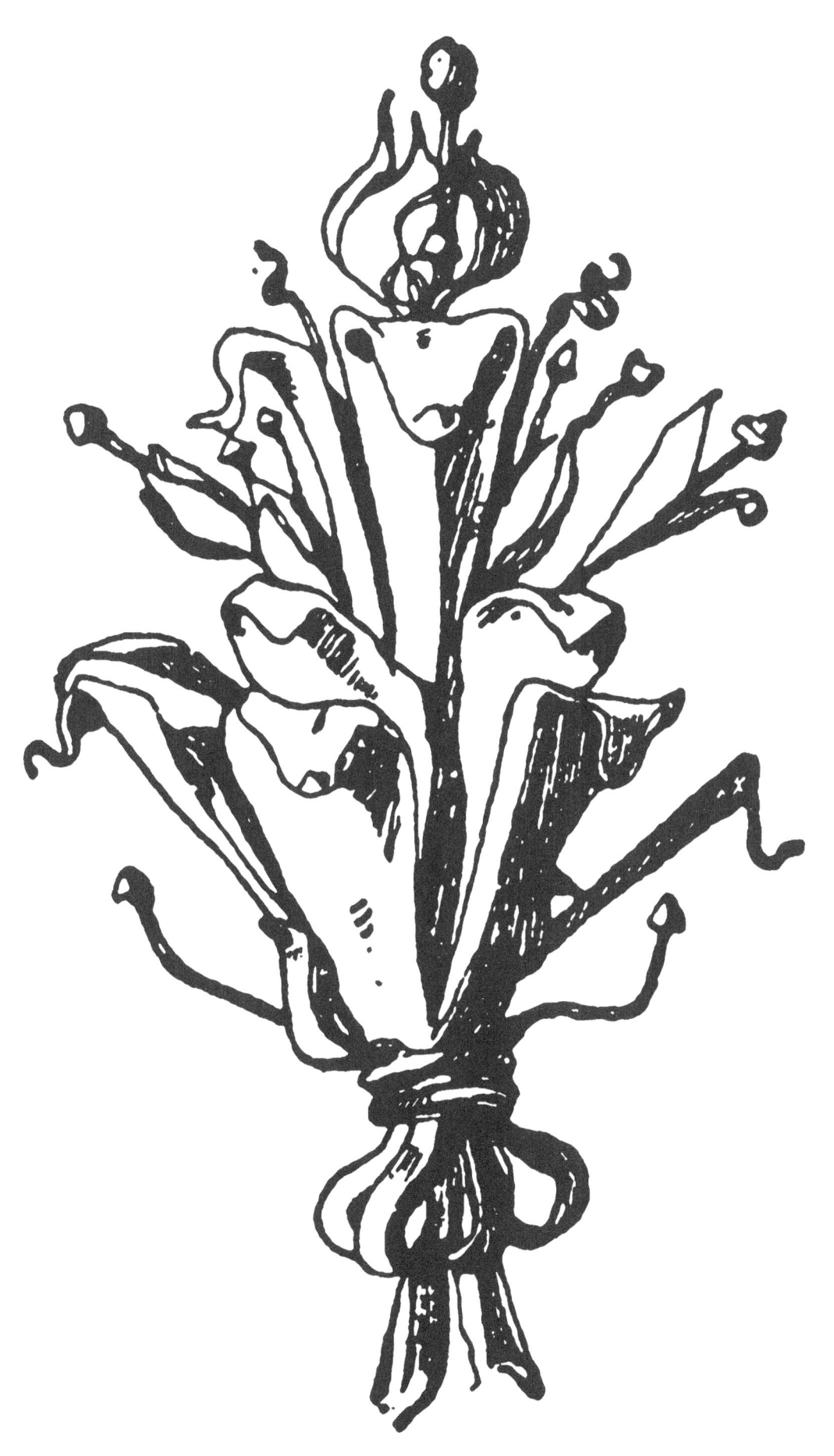

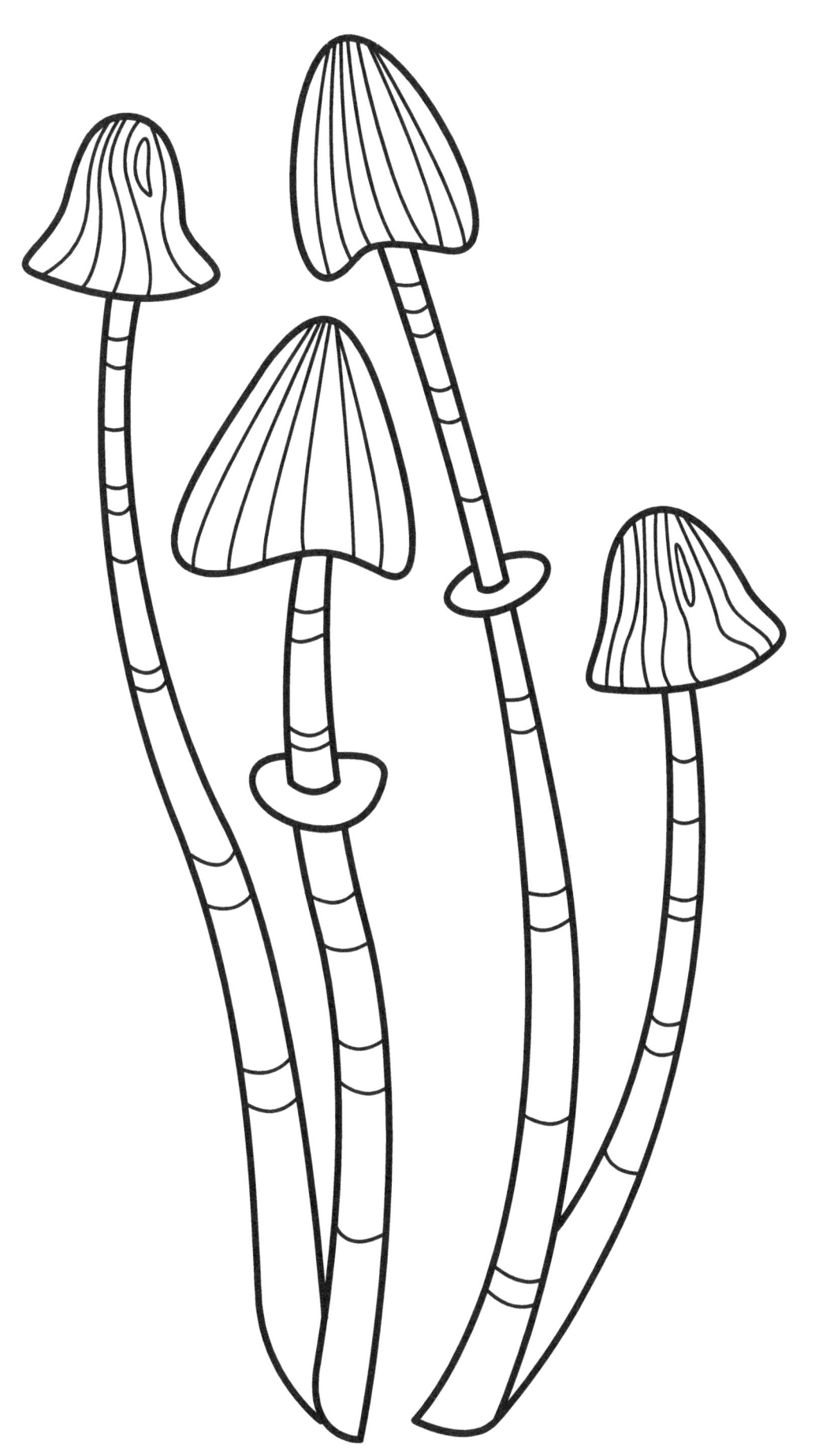

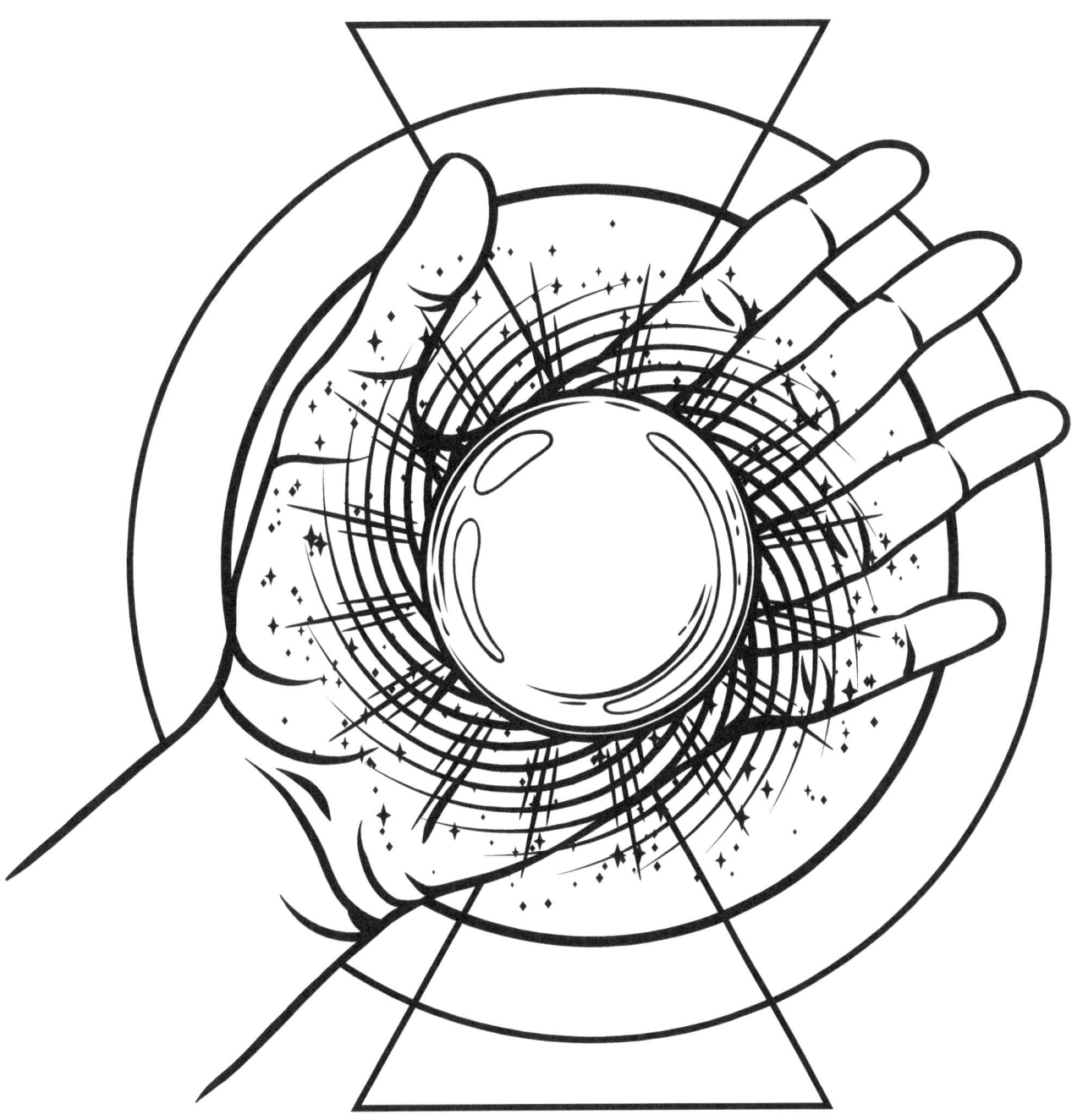

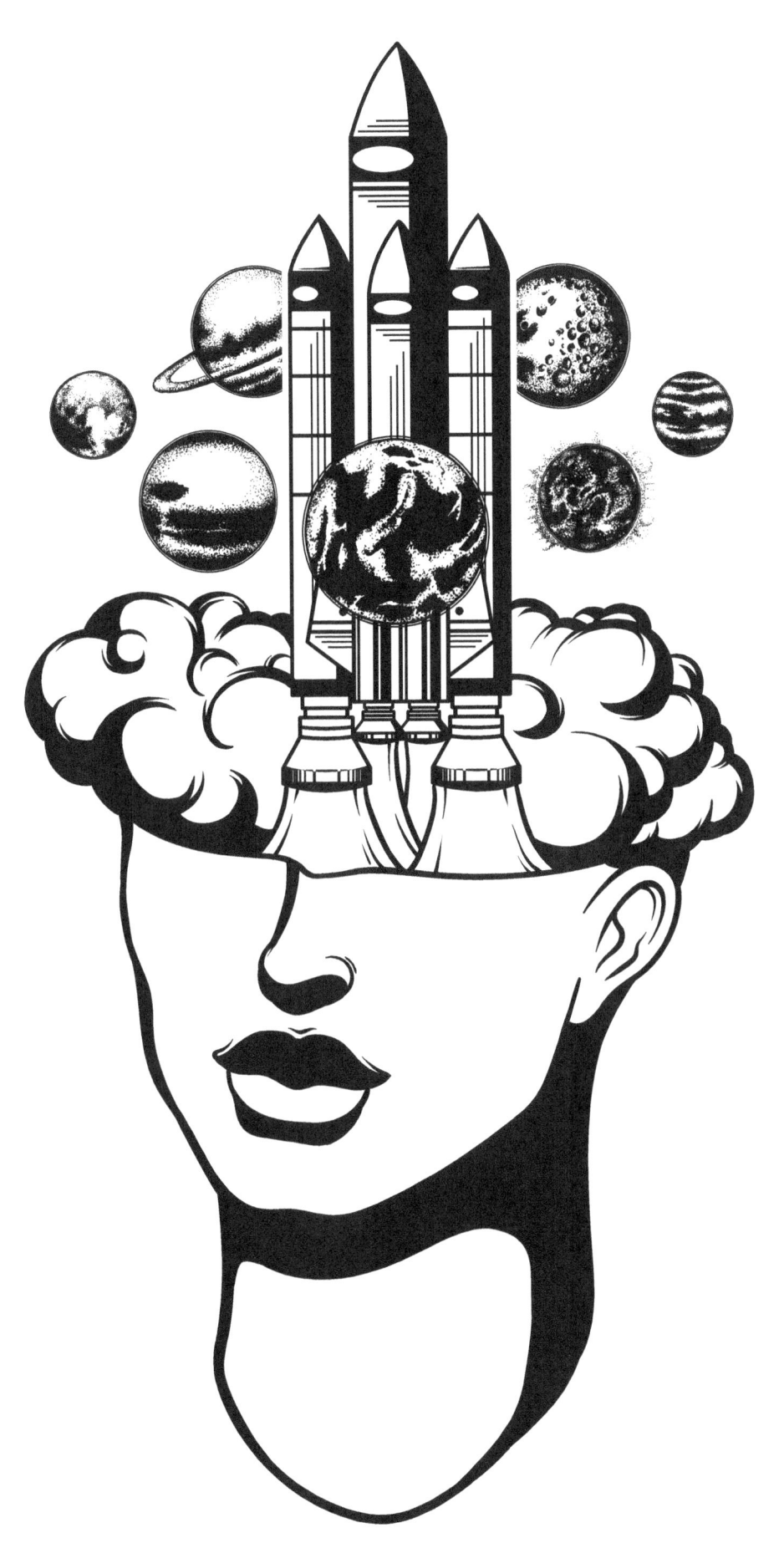

www.ingramcontent.com/pod-product-compliance
Lightning Source LLC
Chambersburg PA
CBHW080849220526
45467CB00008B/2442